I0840923

How to be on Time
for
Time Travelers

D.H. MUDGE

ISBN-10: 1727027051
ISBN-13: 978-1727027051

DEDICATION

For all those husbands, wives, boyfriends, girlfriends, friends, co-workers, managers, or just mild acquaintances waiting patiently for that person to arrive.

CONTENTS

ACKNOWLEDGMENTS

To my wife Amy, one of the many people who inspired me to write this. And to my good friend Wayne Hanson, who showed me how.

PREAMBLE

We are all travelers moving through time. This common action does not require a time machine. However, this book has been written for *both* types of time travelers: those without time machines and those with.

A rule may be given for how to be on time without a machine, followed by a similar rule or additional data for those with a machine. This will be introduced by the italics *"When using a time machine ..."*

INTRODUCTION

For over 30 years my work has required punctuality. For 15 years I ran public classes every business day and I was never late. For another 10 years, I scheduled and directed more than 2,500 demonstrations and I was late only once.

Mistakes do happen and I have been late a few other times. But out of thousands and thousands of appointments, I have a 99.999 percent record of being on time. That means statistically, I have been late once out of every 1,000 appointments. I have probably done better than that, but that is good enough for anyone and that is my qualification for writing this book.

The moral is: *you don't have to be late*. I don't care how busy you are. Being on time is much more important than you might think – or maybe you already know that, but can't seem to do it.

This book contains things you can do to

improve your ability to be on time. Strictly followed, you will also be on time 99.999 percent of the time.

As the person reading this book at this moment, you may not have any trouble with being on time. However, you may know a relative or friend who is constantly late. You can use this book to help them out and I encourage you to do so.

When using a time machine:

While I am not the most experienced time traveler with a machine, I have done my fair share and so feel qualified to give a few important tips. However, the focus of this book is on being on time in the current time rather than using a machine.

Using a machine to "be on time" probably deserves its own separate book which may be issued at a later time.

1.
BASICS

While there are few acceptable reasons to be late, there are many reasons to be on time. One of the most important is manners. It is simply good manners to be on time which is often important to others and can affect their opinion of you. Perhaps this is weakening in today's society, but it is still there and still important. There are also more important reasons. If you are a heart surgeon, there are occasions when you must be on time for an operation or the patient will die. Probably you are not a heart surgeon, but there are still important reasons for you to be on time and for you to control time.

Manners are defined by the *Oxford American Dictionary* as: *"polite or well-bred social behavior."*

There are many times when this counts. Fred is five minutes late to a job interview.

Fred is an excellent candidate with excellent qualifications, but he just got a strike against him, or maybe two, depending on the sensitivities of the interviewers and the job for which he is applying. But, it is always at least one strike and an unnecessary one.

I have interviewed many people for jobs and being on time makes a big difference to me. It tells me three things at least:

1. the person has some control of their life;

2. the person has a sense of good manners;

3. the person has some respect for me which is important, especially if I am going to be their boss.

I'm not saying I wouldn't hire someone just because they were a little late for their first interview, but it could make a difference if it were a close decision between them and someone who was on time.

On the other hand, being early is generally considered a desirable quality. I know of no instance where someone was early to an appointment or activity in which that person was chastised or otherwise penalized.

Besides job interviews, it is important to be on time for many other events. Appointments with clients, presentations, work, classes, catching a plane, train, or bus are a few examples.

There are times when it is less important such as going to a party or an informal affair. If you arrive a few minutes late, no one cares and they are just as happy (we hope) to see you. Going to a movie, some people don't care if they miss the coming attractions, but others do.

There is no psychological introspection in this book on reasons people are chronically late. I don't care about those and neither should you. You might discover a few things about yourself as we go through this and that is okay. Maybe you were brought up with carelessness about time. But, for whatever reason, being late has become a habit for you.

And that is the first thing you should know: we are talking about a habit. The *Oxford American Dictionary* defines "habit" as: "*A settled or regular tendency or practice, especially one that is hard to give up."*

When using a time machine:

The above information is not that applicable as it is highly doubtful that you will be using a time machine for a job interview. And while controlling time is even more important with a machine, it is also generally unlikely that others are expecting you to arrive at a certain time. Most time machine traveling that I am aware of is done for adventure, interest, or fact gathering.

2.
BREAKING THE HABIT

Being late can be hard to give up. You get so you accept that it is just the way you are. It is possible to overcome the habit, however there will be withdrawals in doing so. There are withdrawals from any habit or addiction. You could even miss being late and start wanting to be late again, but that is all part of the withdrawals.

The withdrawals can be mental, emotional and even physical reactions. Some can be slight and some can be very heavy. It depends on the habit and the addiction and the person. A good clue is when you start thinking of why it is okay to be late – you are going through withdrawals.

You have become a genius at thinking up reasons and excuses for being late. You even start thinking of those excuses before you are late because you know you are always late. You probably can think of many excuses you have used. To be on time, you can't use any of them.

You might think that you can just apologize and then everything will be okay and in some instances that may be true. But it may not be true for a job interview, appointments with clients, colleagues, or even friends.

Note: They may say it is fine that you were late, but they don't really think it is fine and right there you lose respect and credibility from those people.

The next thing to know is that *you have the ability to be on time* and you probably already know that. If you are capable of reading this book then you are capable of being on time. You also have to *want* to be on time. If you don't want to be on time, then you probably aren't even reading this book, unless you want someone else to be on time.

So, the first step to being on time is knowing you can do it. This falls under the category of positive thinking and is the first step to achieving anything.

The thing to do right now as you are reading this is: *decide if you want to be on time.* And if you do, then decide *that you can be on time.* If you can't make those decisions, then at least decide that *maybe* you can be on time. If you can't do that, then it is likely that reading the rest of this book won't do you any good. So please, before reading any further, make up your mind that it is at least possible that you can start being on time.

When using a time machine:

Time traveling with a machine requires even stricter discipline. If you can't be on time for regular reasons, then it is doubtful you will be successful as a traveler into the past or future. I strongly suggest that you do not attempt to use a time machine until you have been able to consistently be on time in the present.

3.
WHAT IS TIME?

The Oxford dictionary defines time as *"the continued progress of existence and events in the past, present, and future regarded as a whole."*

Time continues to march forward. It is an inexorable fact of life. *The Oxford American Dictionary* defines "inexorable" as *"impossible to stop or prevent."*

So when you are dealing with time, you are dealing with one of the most powerful forces in life. You may not have thought about it that way, but there it is.

Just because time is so powerful doesn't mean you can't exert control over it and you already do so every day. You can say time controls your life or you can say you control the time in your life. However you say it, time is intimate with everything you do. It is not just about going to work on time, or making it to an appointment on time, it is much more than that.

Here are some obvious examples. You wake up in the morning. If it is a weekday and you are a student or have a job, the *time* you wake up is an important factor. So the very first thing you do each day has to do with time and just about everything after does too. You go to work or class and need to be there at a certain time. You have a project or paper that needs to be done by a certain time. Your days revolve around *when* you do things and anytime we say "when" we are talking about time.

A basic way to describe time is to say that it is the passage of things from one point of existence to another. It has been going on for a very long time and is not likely to end any time soon.

For simplicity's sake, we will say that the time we are talking about in this book is the notation by a clock or calendar as to when something takes place, such as: "The movie starts at 7:00 p.m." Since we have all been reading clocks since we were little that much should be clear.

Just in case you have ever wondered, the initials "p.m." stand for the Latin words *post meridiem* meaning "after noon" and a.m. stands for *ante meridiem* meaning "before noon"

When using a time machine:

All the above applies equally well when using a time machine. You are simply bypassing the normal flow of time and advancing or regressing through time just like you can jump ahead or back in a book. You may not get all the data in between, but you still arrive at the same point, just faster.

4.
DEFINITIONS AND RULES

To many people, "being on time" means "arriving around the time they were supposed to." For example, if the person arrives five minutes past the time, they figure they are still on time. Perhaps the person reading this book right now agrees with this and perhaps there are times when being five or ten minutes late or even later is acceptable. But those times are rare and are generally social events as mentioned earlier.

For the purposes of this book and for most professional activities: *Being on time means arriving at the designated place by the time that has been agreed upon.*

Arriving before the agreed upon time does not violate the definition of being on time as long as one is still at the designated place at the agreed upon time.

Arriving after the agreed upon time is the definition of being late and does violate the definition of being on time no matter the cause.

Examples:

1. The appointment (class, job, whatever) is for 1:00 p.m. at 2312 Barkley Street, Room 404. You arrive at Room 404 at 12:55 p.m. At 12:58 p.m., you go to the bathroom and come back to Room 404 at 1:01 p.m. *You are late.*

2. The appointment is for 2:00 p.m. at Joe's Coffee Shop. You arrive at Joe's Coffee Shop at 1:45 p.m. and wait there for 15 minutes without leaving. *You are on time.*

A very important factor is that to be in control of your time, you must put *attention* on time. To neglect that would be like driving a car without any attention on the car. You would soon be in a wreck.

When using a time machine:

"Being on time" simply means arriving at the time that you previously designated and generally doesn't involve other people unless you have agreed to

meet someone at an earlier or later time. It doesn't necessarily include the place as part of the definition. Arriving at a place in time requires additional understanding which will be covered later.

To put attention on time, you must be aware of *what the time is now* and that is one of the most important things about being on time and it is rule number one:

1. You must know *what the time is now*. This includes knowing what day it is and its date, as in: "4:25 p.m. Tuesday, July 12, 2019."

This is followed by rule number two:

2. You must know *the time of the appointment*. This includes knowing the correct day and time of the appointment as in "9:30 a.m. Thursday, July 21, 2019."

In order to do those things, you must know how to tell time and have easy access to an accurate clock and calendar. There are some people who are not so good at telling time and reading calendars. If you are one of them, you might as well admit it, at least to yourself and work on learning those things.

Even if you can tell time with ease, you can still make a mistake by thinking today is a different day than it is or the day and time of the appointment is on a different day and time.

Many breakdowns of being on time occur just because of violation of the two rules above. These can be remedied by ensuring easy access to accurate clocks and calendars, knowing how to read them, and following the two rules above.

When using a time machine:

The above two rules are also very important in using a machine. You must be able to tell time extremely well particularly the time you are traveling to in the past or the future. However, the first rule of using a time machine is:

1. Get a time machine that works.

I could assume you already have a time machine or you wouldn't bother reading this part, but maybe you are just thinking of getting one. If you do get one, make sure it works.

2. To be on time with a machine, you must know

how to work its controls.
You must know how to do things like:
a) set the controls for the time you want to go to,
b) set the controls for returning to the present,
c) how to turn the machine on and off.

If you don't know how to do these things, then you better learn. If there is no manual with the machine, get proper instruction from somebody who knows how to work the machine you have. Practice many times taking short jumps before you do anything more adventurous.

5.
PREDICTING TIME

Being on time has a lot to do with prediction. You have to be able to predict how long it will take to get from where you are to the place you want to go. It is here also that you can run into a lot of trouble.

You say to yourself that it will take you fifteen minutes to get to Bill's house and you are supposed to be at Bill's house at 4:00 p.m., so you can leave your house at 3:45 p.m. You have just made a big mistake. Maybe it really does take fifteen minutes to get to Bill's house, but did you include putting on your coat, walking out to the car, starting the car, does the car have enough gas, and so on. And what about that last thing you want to do just before you leave?

Well, if you have trouble being on time, I guarantee that you are not thinking of those things. And this leads us to the most important rule in this whole book:

3. To be on time, *you have to be early.*

You may think that doesn't make any sense. But it is a rule that works and that is more important. If you are always trying to be at the appointed place at the appointed time, you are probably late at least 50 percent of the time. If you are working to be at the place before the appointed time, then you will be mostly on time.

If you apply rule number three, there is no reason for you to read another word in this book and you will be successful with being on time.

If you plan to just be on time, there are many things that can get in your way: a slow driver in front of you, you have to wait for a train, the car has trouble starting, too many stop lights, it's raining or snowing, etc., etc.

If someone is going with you or you are depending on someone or something else to get you there, that is a whole new bag of worms. Therefore the next rule:

4. The more people connected with you being on time, *the more difficult it becomes.*

And the only way you can overcome

number four is to convince the other people to be early. Have them read this book.

When using a time machine:

3. Same as rule number three above, but more so.

If you are time traveling to witness an event, you want to get there hours to days early as there is more unpredictability and possibility of running into unknown barriers.

There is the story of time traveler Susie Borland who went back to witness the ride of Paul Revere in 1775. Through a slight miscalculation, she landed a couple of miles outside of Lexington, Massachusetts. Walking, she arrived a few minutes after Revere had come and gone. Although herself an expert horsewoman, she did not have time to secure a horse in order to follow him.

If she had arrived a day earlier, she would have had more than enough time to make preparations for his arrival and could have participated in warning the colonists with him.

I hear she tried again later, this time properly early and was able to partake in the desired witnessing and experience. So all is not lost if you fail the first time, but why fail the first time through improper timing?

There are worse consequences due to improper timing. Dan Morrison, wishing to witness the eruption of Mount Vesuvius in the year 79 AD, arrived just an hour before the eruption. He soon realized the great danger he was in as the eruption began just 10 miles from his location. Luckily, he was able to whisk himself out of there in the time machine before being consumed by fire and ash. Unfortunately, there are far worse stories of those who didn't return at all.

4. Same as number four without using a machine, but less so. Most time machine travel does not include more than one or two people and the factor of being on time is less important as long as you plan to be there early enough.

For those who live several hundred years in the future and travel back to experience the 21ˢᵗ century, I understand that it has become a social thing for groups of people. I don't really know much about that as I don't like associating with those people. For one thing, they are unreliable in relating about what's going on in their time. They tend to be opinionated and biased and so less than truthful.

If you want to know what the future is like just go there yourself. I am not going to say too much about it other than technology continues to advance, but some decent human qualities have been lost. People have become increasingly more concerned about their social standing and appearance than adherence to facts. If you are at all aware of what is going on today, that should come as no surprise.

The future might be an okay place to visit, but I wouldn't want to live there. Call me old-fashioned if you like.

6.

AGREEMENTS

Being on time is part of an agreement and so involves at least two or more people. You told someone you would be there at that time or you agreed with someone that you would be there at that time. Almost anytime you break that agreement then you are late. Nobody feels you have broken the agreement if you are early.

There are real agreements and there are social agreements. Example: The party starts at 8:00 p.m. You arrive at 8:05 p.m. Nobody thinks you are late or that you broke an agreement. But that is not the kind of thing we are talking about here.

You told the boss you would meet him at the office at 8:00 a.m. and you got there at 8:12 a.m. You are late. You told your friend you would pick him up at the airport at 3:30 p.m. and you got there at 4:00 p.m. Your friend may still be grateful that you picked him up, but you were late and he knows it and you know it and it makes a difference. Do it a lot and your friends, family, and fellow workers will consider you someone who is always late and that your lateness is an insult to them spoken or unspoken.

You may know others who are late which can be another excuse as to why you are late. You can probably think of those people and ask yourself if you want to be like them on being late.

7.
THINKING BACKWARDS

Here is the next rule:

5. To be on time, *you must be able to think in the future backwards.*

For example: you need to be at a meeting at 10:00 o'clock tomorrow morning. That's in the future, but you have to think backwards from there. Let's say it takes 30 minutes to get there. So 10:00 minus 30 minutes equals 9:30. But, it will take you about 30 minutes to get ready to go to the meeting, so 9:30 minus 30 minutes equals 9:00. Remembering the rule number three, you want to give yourself a 15 minute cushion so 9:00 minus 15 minutes equals 8:45 in the morning.

Now thinking forward into the future: you need to start getting ready at 8:45 and leave at 9:15 and arrive at 9:45 and then you will *most likely* be on time. I say *"most likely"* because I wanted to emphasize the next rule:

6. You won't always be on time *no matter what*.

I am reluctant to give you that rule because you could use it way too much, but I don't want to hide it from you either because you need to know it.

Sometimes – and this should be rare – no matter what you do, you will still be late. That should at most be only one percent of the time. According to that, you can be on time 99 percent of the time. It should be more like 99.99 percent but 99 percent is still a lot better than you have been doing.

Why is this true? Because:
a) anyone can make an occasional mistake,
b) life is not always predictable.

Between a) and b) at most, these combined should only happen once out of 100 times and if it is happening more than that, then you are kidding yourself. You are not actually applying the rules of being on time and have slipped back into bad old habits.

Under b) of course are the unforeseen

occurrences that do on a rare occasion happen such as:

> a) traffic is truly backed up for two hours and even leaving plenty early could not make up for that,
> b) you really did have a flat tire,
> c) your plane was held up due to bad weather,
> d) you really did lose your keys,
> e) you got lost,
> f) some other really bad stuff happened. After all, being on time is not the most important thing in the world.

When using a time machine:

5. It's a time machine, not a travel machine.

Time machines travel in time, not space. If you want to go to London in 1592 to meet Shakespeare and you start the trip in New York, don't expect to see anything but forest and Native Americans. Arriving in New York in 1592 and then traveling to London will be extremely difficult. So, to travel back to 1592 London, start in London.

I have heard there are time machines that are also travel machines, but I don't know about them and so can't advise you. However, I would bet that all the rules apply to them as well.

6. You can't change what happened.

While this rule is not specifically about being on time, it is a very important rule to know and will save you a lot of time. No matter how you try, you can't change what happened in the past. If you have been using a time machine for a while, then you should know this by now.

This answers the paradox of, "If I went back in time and somehow prevented my father and mother from having children, would I still exist?"

The above example is one of the main plot points of the great movie "Back to the Future" starring Michael J. Fox. If you haven't seen it, then you should. The movie portrays Fox going back in time and inadvertently interfering with his father hooking up with his mother. If his mother and father do not get together, then Fox will cease to exist as their son and thus change the future which violates rule number six above. But, that is just a movie and this is real.

If you <u>were</u> able to prevent your mother and father from having children, then you would not be here in the form in which you now exist. Therefore, you did not and will not succeed in doing that. Something will prevent you. You get lost, your efforts backfire, you break a leg, you just can't do it because it seems so *wrong; who knows what will happen? It doesn't matter how many times you try, you will fail and this has been proven over and over and is an existential fact and you can't change that without changing the very laws of this universe. One could go into all the theories of alternate universes where such things might happen and therefore create universes with alternate timelines, but that is way beyond the scope of this little book.*

In another example, you might want to go back to prevent John Wilkes Booth from shooting Lincoln, but you will never succeed on this particular timeline. However, let's say John Wilkes Booth had a cousin Bob; you might succeed in preventing Bob from doing something.

Perhaps if we were to dig into the past and all the lives of Booth's relatives, we might find that cousin Bob was foiled at robbing a bank by some mysterious stranger (you) who was never seen again. But we don't know that because nobody has done that research and if they have researched all of Booth's cousins, did they research his second cousins because maybe Bob is his second cousin?

If you did foil cousin Bob from robbing the bank, maybe that created many effects in history and maybe one of those effects resulted in the Titanic sinking.

So now you might want to go back and <u>not</u> foil Bob, but you won't be able to do that either and the

Titanic will still sink.

This rule also applies to going back and meeting yourself. For example, you find out the winning lottery numbers after they were drawn today. You then go back a day and tell your former self those numbers. If history shows you did not win the lottery, something will prevent you from winning. Maybe you lose the ticket or it gets destroyed or someone steals it, but whatever happens, you will not win that lottery.

On the other hand, your future self could come back and give you the winning numbers and if history shows you won, then you will win. If nothing else, this should make you suspicious of all lottery winners particularly those who have won more than once.

8.
PLANNING, PLANNING, PLANNING

7. You must be *able to plan*.

Here is where you can find the most excuses and it is really part of rule number five, but more so. This is the one that prevents you from losing your keys because you already have your keys or you made sure you knew where your keys were long before you have to leave.

Planning includes having the right clothes ready, having the correct directions, having the right stuff ready to take and many other possibilities.

If the appointment is a complex affair, then you should have started days or weeks earlier, carefully planning for it which ties into rule number eight.

8. You can never start *too early to get ready.*

Maybe you think that is ridiculous, but that's just because you are late so much. For the very few times that I have been late it is number eight that I have violated and it goes like this: I have to be someplace in four hours and have really no preparation that I need to do other than ensure that I have a folder of information to take with me. I know that the folder is in a file drawer that is 10 feet away so there is no reason to pull out a folder that I won't need for at least three and a half hours so I don't bother with it.

Three and a half hours later I go to the file drawer to get the folder and it is not there. I spend 30 minutes finding the folder and I end up being late.

When you *think* of something to get ready, that is when you should do it because as per rule number eight, you can never start too early to get ready. I will think of something I will need for an appointment and though it seems way too early to get it ready, I will get it ready and I am almost always glad I did and I have never been sad that I did.

When using a time machine:

7. Planning is even more important when using a time machine, particularly if you are going into the future.

When going into the past you can have some prediction since it is easily possible to have some knowledge of when and where you are going. You should be able to plan what clothes to wear, the type of money you will need, and the language to speak.

Going into the future is a whole lot less predictable and there are many factors that should be considered when doing so. The farther you go, the less you will know. Climate obviously changes, the terrain can change, whole cultures and languages rise and fall. So be prepared for anything.

I have heard there are future road maps available that give some details of things like future cultures, climate, and terrain, but I haven't seen any.

9.

THE TOUGHEST CHALLENGE

You can follow all the rules given here perfectly and do everything necessary to be on time, but you may still fail because of what might be the toughest factor for you to overcome.

You are married to or otherwise partnered with someone who is always late and doesn't care. You can try to coax the person to be on time, but that just ends up in a quarrel or being ignored. You can plead and beg, but that probably won't do any good either. Getting mad just makes it worse. Or, you can listen to their explanations about being late and if you really listen and acknowledge them without trying to make them feel guilty or wrong that sometimes can help a lot.

Then you can gently work with them to use some of the rules given such as number three and possibly over time it will improve, but that depends on how well you treat the other person and how willing they are to change. You can show them this book too and that is the best you can do.

However, doing the above rules will get you well on the road to being on time and it will change your life.

EPILOGUE

As I re-read this small book, I feel I have covered the subject of being on time in the present adequately. However, I believe I gave being on time with a machine less than satisfactory coverage.

I started out writing this with the idea of only covering the present time, but as I progressed, I decided to add a bit of what I know using a time machine as some might find that useful too. I could have done a lot more, but I am not certain of the amount of interest it would have since at this time only a few individuals are involved with using a machine and I know most of them.

If I am incorrect in my estimation and there is greater interest than I am aware of on using a time machine, please let me know. If there is enough interest, I will consider writing an expanded volume on the subject. You can do this by either noting it on the website where you purchased this book or submitting a letter to the bookstore where you bought it.

Thank you,

D.H. Mudge

2019

LISTS

You can use the following checklists to help you be on time.

Checklist #1: How to be on Time

1. What time is it now?

2. What time is the appointment?

3. Where is the location of the appointment?

4. Do you have accurate directions to that location?

5. By what means (car, bus, train, friend, etc.) will you be getting to that location?

6. From where you will be starting, how long on average does it take to get to that location?

7. Is there anything you must do prior to leaving? Examples: get gas, make a phone call, buy new shoes, etc.

8. What are you taking with you to the appointment? Examples: a briefcase, a folder of

information, a smart phone, a computer, etc.

9. Do you know exactly where the items are located <u>now</u> that you will be taking with you?

10. Check to make sure those items are where you think they are - use rule #8: You can never start *too early to get ready.*

 11. Do you know what clothes you will be wearing?

12. Are those clothes ready for you to wear?

13: Think backwards to determine the time you need to leave – use rule #3: To be on time, *you have to be early.*

14: Is there someone else you have to contact to make sure you will be on time?

15: Is there someone else going with you that you need to ensure is also on time?

16: What else do you have to have ready? Examples: car keys, photos, computer, data, tools, etc.

Checklist #2: How to be on Time Using a Time Machine

1. Is the machine working and ready to go?

2, Use the systems test procedure to ensure functionality. Most machines have them. If yours doesn't, at least test it to make sure it will turn on and power up.

3. Are you familiar enough with the machine to be using it?

4. Have you done simple test runs like going back an hour earlier or an hour later?

5. Have you worked out your exact time and location of departure?

6. Do you have the exact date and time that you want to travel to?

7. Are you in the right location to where you want to go?

8. If you will have to travel from the location you arrive at, have you allowed for enough time for that travelling?

9. What method of traveling do you need to do once you have arrived at your selected time?

10. Do you have the right clothes for where and when you are going?

11. Do you have the right money for where and when you are going?

12. Do you know the right language for where and when you are going?

13. What else do you need to take with you? Examples: tools, maps, directions, compass, extra clothes, etc.

14. If someone else is involved, do they understand what is happening and what they will need?

Note: Both lists should be used when operating a time machine.

ABOUT THE AUTHOR

When D.H. Mudge isn't busy traveling
in time and space, he is busy writing
more books.

He lives with his family in California.

www.ingramcontent.com/pod-product-compliance
Lightning Source LLC
Chambersburg PA
CBHW061734250726